This book is dedicated to the amazing
human beings that care for the homeless
animals at Animal Rescue, Inc., located in
New Freedom, Pennsylvania.

$1.00 was donated to Animal Rescue, Inc. when you purchased this book.
If you are interested in helping further, please check out their website at
www.animalrescueinc.org.

Illustrations by Nejla Shojaie
Book Design by Praise Saflor

Publisher's Cataloging-in-Publication data

Names: Michal, Zoe Alexa, author. | Shojaie, Nejla, illustrator.
Title: All grandparents love their grandbabies / Zoe Alexa Michal ; illustrated by Nejla Shojaie.
Series: Baby Love
Description: Baltimore, MD: Give Back Books, LLC, 2021. | Summary: A rhyming picture book displaying the love
grandparent animals have for their grandbabies.
Identifiers: LCCN: 2021915746 | ISBN: 978-1-7374250-5-2 (hardcover) | 978-1-7374250-6-9 (paperback)
Subjects: LCSH Animals--Infancy--Juvenile fiction. | Animals--Juvenile fiction. | Grandparents--Juvenile
fiction. | CYAC Animals--Infancy--Fiction. | Animals--Fiction. | Grandparents--Fiction. | BISAC JUVENILE
FICTION / Animals / Baby Animals | JUVENILE FICTION / Animals / Mammals | JUVENILE FICTION /
Bedtime & Dreams | JUVENILE FICTION / Family / Multigenerational
Classification: LCC PZ7.1.M5158 All 2021 | DDC [E]--dc23

ALL Grandparents Love Their Grandbabies

Written by Zoe Michal

Illustrated by Nejla Shojaie

Cat grandparents love their grandkittens.

They love their soft fluffy fur

and the sound of their purr.

They love their twisty tail that is soft and long

and their pink, sticky, prickly tongue.

They love all the places they can reach

and even the sounds of their high-pitched screech.

Yes, cat grandparents love their grandkittens from the very start—

every minute, every day, with all of their hearts.

Dolphin grandparents love their grandcalves.

They love their smooth and rubbery sensitive skin

and their pectoral flippers and dorsal fin.

They love that they eat thirty-three pounds of fish each day

and that they like to do acrobatic spins and jumps as they play.

They love that they have a blowhole and don't chew their food

and they adore their long snout and smart aptitude.

Yes, dolphin grandparents love their grandcalves from the very start—

every minute, every day, with all of their hearts.

Giraffe grandparents love their grandcalves.

They love their tiny, flat, fur-covered horns

and their ability to stand on the day they were born.

They love their unique spotted skin

and their fast legs, long and thin.

They love their tongues that are purple and blue

and the way they eat their food and rechew.

Yes, giraffe grandparents love their grandcalves from the very start—

every minute, every day, with all of their hearts.

Rabbit grandparents love their grandkittens.

They love their hoppy twists when they're happy

and their ears that are soft, long, and flappy.

They love their soft fur and twitching nose

and their twenty-eight teeth that continually grow.

They love that they are hard to catch

and will use their teeth and claws to scratch.

Yes, rabbit grandparents love their grandkittens from the very start—

every minute, every day, with all of their hearts.

Horse grandparents
love their grandfoals.

They love their big eyes on the sides of their head,

and that they can stand or sleep when they are ready for bed.

They love their thick muscles and their powerful lungs

that help make them fast and incredibly strong.

They love that they eat apples, carrots, and hay

and their sounds of braying, whinny, and neigh.

Yes, horse grandparents love their grandfoals from the very start—

every minute, every day, with all of their hearts.

Hedgehog grandparents
love their grandhoglets.

They love their adorable face and small black nose,

and that they enjoy belly rubs while in a particular pose.

They love that they can curl up into a ball with their quills sticking out

and that they sometimes chirp when they are hungry and pout.

They love that their favorite foods are snails and slugs

and that they'll eat other things, but they prefer to eat bugs!

Yes, hedgehog grandparents love their grandhoglets from the very start—

every minute, every day, with all of their hearts.

Dog grandparents love their grandpuppies.

They love their cute faces and puppy-dog eyes

and the sound of their bark and sweet little cries.

They love the feel of their wet and cold black snoot,

and correcting them when they destroy a shoe or a boot.

They love their tails that wiggle and wag

and the jingling sound of their silver dog tag.

Yes, dog grandparents love their grandpuppies from the very start—

every minute, every day, with all of their hearts.

Cow grandparents love their grandcalves.

They love counting their baby teeth—up to thirty-two!—
and the sound of their grandcalf saying, "Moo! Moo!"
They love their long tails that display how they feel
and their diet of grass that they eat as their meal.
They love their birth weight of sixty to one hundred pounds,
and the spots on their skin of white, black, and brown.
Yes, cow grandparents love their grandcalves from the very start—
every minute, every day, with all of their hearts.

Zebra grandparents love their grandfoals.

They love their white fur with brown or black stripes

and their ability to protect each other with very strong bites.

They love their thick, long and black eyelashes

and their diet of shrubs, leaves, and various grasses.

They love their striped mane on the top of their back

and their willingness to help friends who are under attack.

Yes, zebra grandparents love their grandfoals from the very start—

every minute, every day, with all of their hearts.

Sloth grandparents
love their grandcubs.

They love their constant look of a smiling face

and that they could never win a running race.

They love that they pee pee and poo poo only once a week

and the sound of their high-pitch squeaking and shriek.

They love their long claws and incredible swimming skill,

and that they only love warm weather, never a chill.

Yes, sloth grandparents love their grandcubs from the very start—

every minute, every day, with all of their hearts.

Chipmunk grandparents love their grandpups.

They love that they hold food in their chubby cheeks

and their high-pitched voice with its talkative speak.

They love their stripes on their face and back

and their quickness to get away when under attack.

They love their fur color of reddish shades, gray, and brown

and the way they dig their burrows deep underground.

Yes, chipmunk grandparents love their grandpups from the very start—

every minute, every day, with all of their hearts.

 **E**lephant grandparents
love their grandcalves.

They love their eyelashes that can grow up to five inches long

and their trunk of seven feet that is extremely strong.

They love that they eat up to two hundred pounds of food each day

and use their trunks to suck up water and spray.

They love the loud sound of their trumpet and thick, wrinkly skin

and their tusks used for digging and their tails long and thin.

Yes, elephant grandparents love their grandcalves from the very start—

every minute, every day, with all of their hearts.

Penguin grandparents love their little grandchicks.

They love that they're a bird but cannot fly

and that they jump in the air before taking a dive.

They love their black-and-white colors and waddling walk,

and their big, webbed feet and high-pitched squawk.

They love how they slide on their bellies and have no teeth

and that they walk on the ice and go swimming beneath.

Yes, penguin grandparents love their grandchicks from the very start—

every minute, every day, with all of their hearts.

Pig grandparents love their grandpiglets.

They love that they have big ears and small eyes

and that they come in a large and a tinier size.

They love that they are clean and do not sweat

and that sometimes they are even a favorite pet!

They love that they have four hoofs with four toes

and that they sleep side by side or nose to nose.

Yes, pig grandparents love their grandpiglets from the very start—

every minute, every day, with all of their hearts.

Place Photo of
Grandparents and Grandchild

Human Grandparents love their grandbabies.

They love that freshly clean smell on the top of their head,

and the first night they sleep all night in their bed.

They love their ten little fingers and ten little toes,

and their ability to wear the smallest of clothes.

They love the sound of their sweet coos and delicate touch,

and the feeling that they could love someone so much!

Yes, human grandparents love their grandbabies from the very start—

every minute, every day, with all of their hearts.

For more information:

www.gbbooks.org
contact author: zoe.michal@gbbooks.org

We hope that you enjoy this book and
leave a review on Amazon.
www.amazon.com/author/zoemichal

For freebies from Give Back Books (coloring and activity pages), scan the QR Code below:

Made in the USA
Middletown, DE
07 December 2021

54526778R00020